CONFUCIANISM

ORIGINS • BELIEFS • PRACTICES
HOLY TEXTS • SACRED PLACES

CONFUCIANISM

ORIGINS • BELIEFS • PRACTICES
HOLY TEXTS • SACRED PLACES

Jennifer Oldstone-Moore

OXFORD
UNIVERSITY PRESS

2177626

Oxford University Press

Oxford   New York
Auckland   Bangkok   Buenos Aires   Cape Town   Chennai
Dar es Salaam   Delhi   Hong Kong   Istanbul   Karachi   Kolkata
Kuala Lumpur   Madrid   Melbourne   Mexico City   Mumbai   Nairobi
São Paolo   Shanghai   Singapore   Taipei   Tokyo   Toronto

and associated companies in
Berlin

First published in the United States of America in 2002 by
Oxford University Press, Inc.
198 Madison Avenue, New York, N.Y. 10016–4314
Oxford is a registered trademark of Oxford University Press

Conceived, created, and designed by
Duncan Baird Publishers, London, England

Library of Congress Cataloging-in-Publication Data
Oldstone-Moore, Jennifer.
  Confucianism: origins, beliefs, practices, holy texts, sacred place/Jennifer Oldstone-Moore
    p. cm.
  Includes bibliographical references and index.
  ISBN 0-19-521908-2
    1. Confucianism. I. Title.

BL1853.O44 2002
299'.512–dc21   2002072269

ISBN: 0-19-521908-2

Project Editor: Christopher Westhorp
Senior Editor: Diana Loxley
Design: Cobalt id
Picture Researcher: Julia Ruxton

Typeset in Garamond Three
Color reproduction by Scanhouse, Malaysia
Printed and bound in Singapore by Imago

NOTES
The abbreviations BCE and CE are used throughout this book:
BCE Before the Common Era (the equivalent of BC)
CE Common Era (the equivalent of AD)

10 9 8 7 6 5 4 3 2 1

Page 2: Worshipers lighting incense as an act of veneration at the Confucian
temple in the ancient city of Quanzhou. The temple structure dates from the
12th–13th century Southern Song dynasty.

CONTENTS

INTRODUCTION

Confucianism—along with the other two formal traditions, Daoism and Buddhism, as well as the pervasive
popular religion—has been one of the most influential
systems of thought in China for centuries and remains an
important aspect of Chinese civilization. It formed the
basis of imperial ideology and was reflected in sacred
rites of the emperor to ensure harmony between human
beings and the cosmos, and in the examinations for the
selection of his administrators. It also underlay social
and family ethics and the rites of ancestor veneration.
The tradition spread with Chinese cultural and political
domination to Korea, Vietnam, and Japan, and to communities of East Asian immigrants worldwide. Just as in
China, it functions in these other cultural contexts as one
part of a complex of religious traditions, all of which
may be seen as complementary rather than exclusive.

The Confucian tradition actually began well before
Confucius (the latinate form of Kong Fuzi, "Master
Kong"), and is known in Chinese as *rujia*, or the "School
of the Ru," *ru* meaning "weak" or "yielding." *Ru* also
referred to the learned aristocracy of the defeated Shang
dynasty (ca. 1766–1050BCE), who nevertheless continued to serve as specialists in *li* (ritual and protocol)—
that is, in determining appropriate behavior and

A 17th-century calligrapher's brush-rest, which represents the world in miniature, comprehensible form, with the five sacred mountains that mark out its center and each compass point.

techniques of government. The willingness of the *ru* to serve their conquerors appears to have been motivated at least in part by their devotion to the *li*. Over time, *ru* came to refer to one trained in the *li* who worked in the government, and was later used more loosely to refer to an educated person. The layers of meanings of this term—including devotion to *li*, motivation by virtue, service to government, and dedication to education—have been key components of what, according to Confucian tradition, constitutes the ideal person.

Confucianism is premised on the idea of a natural hierarchy, which is believed to be the ordering principle of all things and is reflected in ancient Chinese cosmology. This cosmology expresses two fundamental principles: the cosmos is a sacred place; and all aspects of it are interrelated. The central purpose of Chinese religion in general is to uphold this sacredness by maintaining harmony among human beings and between humanity and nature. The focus of Confucianism in particular is on creating harmony in human society. According to the ancient understanding of how the cosmos functions, everything that exists, including Heaven, Earth, human beings, and deities, is made up of the same vital substance, or *qi* (*ch'i*). *Qi* is manifested most basically as two complementary forces, *yin* and *yang*. *Yin* denotes that which is dark, moist, inert, turbid, cold, soft, and feminine, and *yang* denotes that which is bright, dry, growing, light, warm, hard, and masculine. All things consist of both *yin* and *yang* in varying proportions.

The *yin-yang* view of the cosmos functions in conjunction with the cycle of the "Five Phases," which furnishes a more detailed structure for understanding how vital forces interact. The phases are represented by "fire," "wood," "metal," "water," and "earth," but rather than being material elements, these are to be understood as metaphysical forces, each exercising a dominating influence at any one time. Everything in the universe—the changes and patterns in nature, the heavenly bodies, time, natural phenomena, and human society—is linked by its participation in cycles of transformation as well as by its varying proportions of *yin* and *yang*.

The action of *yin* and *yang* and the Five Phases are the primal and cosmic patterns that inform human relationships. The teachings of Confucianism are the means by which those human relationships are fulfilled, bringing them into line with cosmic patterns, which will, in a ripple effect, bring harmony to all of society and, ultimately, to the cosmos. In practice, these social patterns are seen most basically in the "Five Relationships" (see p.55–7), especially the relationship between parent and child, which is typified by the Confucian ethic of *xiao*, or filial piety, and in statecraft, which presumed the domination of a benevolent and virtuous ruler over obedient and receptive subjects. Confucian statecraft was the basis of government in East Asia for centuries, disappearing in its official form early in the twentieth century. Although Confucianism is no longer used as state ideology today, it remains a distinctive feature in the life and mores of the region.

CHAPTER ONE

ORIGINS AND HISTORICAL DEVELOPMENT

The Confucian tradition began in Chinese antiquity, many centuries before the birth of Confucius. It was interpreted by classical Confucians and then reformulated in the Han dynasty (206BCE–220CE), creating a powerful imperial ideology. The Neo-Confucian movement that arose during the Song dynasty (960–1279CE) expanded Confucian concerns and established new methods for the attainment of enlightenment.

Due to China's political and cultural dominance in East Asia, Confucianism had a lasting impact in Japan, Vietnam, and Korea—territories well beyond the north Chinese heartland of its origin. Its influence continues to the present day in these cultures, with social harmony and responsibility stressed above individual freedom and rights.

LEFT: Huang Di, the Yellow Emperor, is the semi-mythical forefather of the Chinese people and propagator of Chinese culture (see pages 12 and 44). It was ancient, heroic figures such as Huang Di who became exemplars of virtuous behavior and kingship.

Confucian ideals and practices were not initiated by the figure Confucius himself, but have their roots many centuries before his existence, in Chinese antiquity in the Yellow River valley, where the legendary Yellow Emperor is said to have established Chinese culture. Myth apart, the hallmarks of Confucianism—ancestor veneration, sacrifice, and a religio-political order—are evident in the earliest Chinese written records, the Shang oracle-bone inscriptions, which were discovered at Anyang in northeast China.

Divination with "oracle bones" was an important practice during the Shang dynasty (ca. 1766–1050BCE) and was adopted by the royal house in order to receive supernatural guidance on a range of concerns, from forecasting the weather and determining the cause of a toothache, to the right time to wage war, the likelihood of success in hunting, and the abundance of the harvest.

Although questions were sometimes put to the supreme being known as Shang Di, the "Lord on High," by far the greatest percentage of oracles was addressed to ancestors, who were believed to be a source of blessing or misfortune, particularly concerning human fertility. At this time only royalty was believed to have ancestors; common people's souls decayed with their bodies. These ancestors could be relied on to have the interests of the family—and therefore the state—as their primary concern. Shang Di was usually considered to be too remote from humanity to consult for most mortal concerns. In making the oracle, a question would be intoned as a heated rod was placed on the shoulder-blade of an ox or sheep or the plastron (underside) of a turtle. A diviner would then interpret the cracks made by the hot rod to reveal the answer to the question. The recorded questions and answers disclose the sense of duty and connection presumed between ancestor and descendant.

In the Zhou dynasty (1050–256BCE), Shang Di was largely replaced by Tian, "Heaven," the source of power and order. Heaven was a non-anthropomorphic force that was able to control and influence events. The Zhou proclaimed that they had received the "Mandate of Heaven," the divinely sanctioned right to rule, because of their virtue in contrast to the depravity of the last Shang rulers. The idea that virtue and beneficent rule are the basis of the state was thus firmly established by this date.

During the Zhou dynasty, various ritual practices, behavioral codes, literary and poetic works, and exemplary deeds of filiality, loyalty, virtue, and good government were distilled into the canonical work, the "Five Classics," which is traditionally attributed to this period (see pp.34–6). By the sixth century BCE, the political authority of the Zhou rulers had declined, and the ensuing period of disorder saw the formulation of numerous theories aimed at restoring harmony and peace—these were collectively known as the "Hundred Schools." It was in this context that Confucius put forth his ideas about order in society and the state. Born in 551BCE at Qufu in modern Shandong province, Confucius (Kong Qiu, also known as Kongzi, "Master Kong") came from a poor but respectable family. After serving in the government of the state of Lu, he spent thirteen years traveling the various Chinese states and asking their rulers to put into practice his ideas about government. He returned home unsuccessful and disappointed and spent the rest of his days, until his death in 479BCE, teaching and, as tradition has it, working on the Five Classics.

Confucius maintained that in order to have a harmonious society and effective government, the primary relationship of parent and child must be in order. The obligations of filial piety—the honor, respect, love, and service owed between parent and child—is a theme which is paralleled in other relationships in society. Good government, for example, consists of a similar process of care and obligation between ruler and subject. All members of society must be sensitive and practiced in what is required of them in their various roles.

Attention to rank, obligations, and ritual duties will lead ultimately to the perfection of oneself and the transformation of society.

Confucius' great follower, Mencius (Mengzi, 371–ca. 289BCE), elaborated Confucius' teachings about human virtue and good government, proclaiming the original goodness of human nature and the right of the people to rebel against a wicked ruler.

The third great Confucian thinker of the classical era, Xunzi (active ca. 298–238BCE) offered a very different view of human nature. He claimed that humans were originally evil and became good only through strict laws and harsh punishments, in addition to attention to ritual. Xunzi's views were implemented by the "Legalists"— another of the "Hundred Schools"—who held that laws and punishment, rather than virtuous example and moral suasion, must be the basis of government. The Legalists have been reviled in Chinese history for their role in the brutal reign (221–209BCE) of the first emperor of all China, Qin Shihuangdi—a period characterized by mass book-burnings and intense suspicion of intellectuals.

The Confucian school did not enjoy official patronage for several centuries after the death of Confucius, and was even persecuted under the Qin dynasty (221–207BCE). It was officially adopted in the Han

A scene from the life of Confucius depicting him with his disciples. Ink and watercolor, Qing dynasty (1644–1911).

dynasty (206BCE–220CE), when the emperor recognized that the rituals promoted by the Confucian literati were a source of impressive court ceremonial and a stabilizing force for society. Despite Confucian criticism of Legalism, Han Confucianism was a distinctive blend of Confucian idealism and Legalist pragmatism, a combination which proved effective for virtually two millennia of Chinese imperial rule. The infrastructure of Confucian rule was created at this time: a national university was established, texts lost during the Qin destruction of books were reconstructed, and a system was put into place whereby "men of talent" (ability and good moral character) were identified, trained in Confucian virtues and literature, and brought into government service. This bureaucratic system became the foundation of civil service selections in imperial China, and continued until the twentieth century; this system was eventually adopted in both Vietnam and Korea.

In addition to making Confucianism the basis of the state, the Han Dynasty promoted scholarship and new trends in Confucian thought. Most notable was the work of Dong Zhongshu, who created a philosophical synthesis that included Confucianism, Legalism, and cosmological theories based on the principles of the two complementary forces, *yin* and *yang* (see pp.8–9). Ancient Chinese cosmology posits that everything is made of *qi* (vital matter, life energy or life force). *Qi* is most basically manifest in *yin* and *yang* and all things are made up of various proportions of *yin qi* and *yang qi*. Dong's genius was to combine these cosmological concepts with Confucian political ideals, forming a triad of Heaven, Earth, and humanity. According to this vision, the ruler was perceived as the pivot between the three, ensuring order and harmony for "all under Heaven."

After the fall of the Han dynasty came several centuries of disunity, characterized by the decline of

Confucianism, the growth of Buddhism, and the expanding popularity of Daoism. Confucianism was revitalized in the Song dynasty (960–1279CE) in a movement known as Neo-Confucianism. This movement was characterized by its expansion of Confucian concerns to include metaphysics and new methods for self-cultivation and enlightenment. The most renowned scholar of this period was Zhu Xi (1130–1200CE). He proposed that all things, including human nature, have an ordering principle, *li* (to be distinguished from the homophone *li*, which means "ritual"), that shapes the vital matter, *qi*. Humans must "investigate things" to understand their underlying principles, and cultivate themselves so as to base their actions on the appropriate human behavior. There are clear Buddhist and Daoist influences in the Neo-Confucian advocacy of "quiet sitting" (meditation) as a technique of self-cultivation that leads to transformative experiences of insight.

A later Neo-Confucian who challenged Zhu Xi's teaching was Wang Yangming (Wang Shouren, 1472–1529). Wang advocated "quiet sitting" as a means to self-knowledge and awareness, and the importance of acting upon one's realizations—these insights were summed up in his theory of the unity of knowledge and action. Wang's claim that "knowledge is the beginning of action, and action is the completion of knowledge" implies that knowledge of something, for example of virtue, necessarily includes acting in a like, in this case virtuous, manner; a knowledge of filial piety means acting in a filial manner, and so on.

Vietnam and Korea came under Confucian influence mainly as a consequence of Chinese conquest during the Han dynasty. This early contact established the pattern of Confucian-based government, and although the degree of Chinese control in the following centuries was variable, Confucian learning and ideology remained integral to the government and culture of the Korean and Vietnamese élite. After the collapse of the Tang dynasty in 907CE, Vietnam to a large extent maintained its political independence from China, but nevertheless continued to adopt and adapt Chinese culture, ruling by means of a Confucian-style bureaucracy staffed through civil service exams based on the Chinese Classics. As early as 427CE, a Korean state adopted a Chinese-style government and bureaucracy. Korea also produced what was in many ways the most thoroughly Confucian state ever: the Choson, or Yi, dynasty (1392–1910). In education, bureaucracy, principles of government, and high culture, the Koreans reproduced a model Confucian civilization. The Choson produced an impressive array of scholars of Neo-Confucianism, the most famous of whom was Yi T'ongye (1501–1570), who developed and expanded on Zhu Xi's philosophy.

The situation in Japan differed from that in Korea or Vietnam. As an island state, the Japanese actively chose—as opposed to being forced to import—Confucian ideas. The first great wave of borrowing came in the sixth century CE, and was part of a movement to centralize authority in the Japanese state while adopting Chinese high culture. Prince Shotoku issued the "Seventeen Article Constitution" in 604CE which laid out the basic elements of a Confucian state, stressing the importance of central authority and social harmony produced by the specific roles to be played by each person. After this initial era of cultural borrowing, Confucianism became a fundamental, though understated, aspect of Japanese culture.

The high point of Confucian scholarship in Japan was during the Tokugawa period (1600–1868). The Tokugawa rulers saw Confucianism as a means of establishing and perpetuating stability after centuries of civil war. Kaibara Ekken (1630–1714) was the leading figure in the promotion of Japanese Neo-Confucianism, and the man who made Confucian ethics accessible to the average Japanese person.

The Confucian states of China, Vietnam, and Korea disappeared in the nineteenth and twentieth centuries due to imperialist encroachment. Many Chinese reformers and radicals, including Communists, blamed Confucianism as the cause of Chinese weakness in the face of imperialist advancement. Others, however, saw it as the basis of East Asian character and morality, and as essential to the success of modernizing nations.

Despite the disappearance of the Confucian state, Confucian ideals have continued to underpin East Asian civilizations. A new wave of Confucian scholars in the twentieth and twenty-first centuries—including Mou Tsung-san, Carsun Chang, and Tu Weiming—has reinterpreted Confucianism in the light of the modern world. The city-state of Singapore under Lee Kuan Yew and the Republic of China on Taiwan have looked to the ideas of Confucianism as being central to morality and social harmony. Finally, Confucianism has been identified as a vital part of the mixture that has contributed to the booming economies of East Asia in recent decades. It is clear that the Confucian tradition remains fundamental to the assumptions and actions of East Asians and, although diffused through family, society, culture, and political structures, is unmistakably present and formative.

Yao, Shun, and Yu in the *Shu Jing* (*Classic of Documents*) and the *Mengzi* (*Mencius*)

❝ Yu said, 'Oh Sovereign, remember this! ... There are water, fire, metal, wood, earth and grain; these must be regulated. There are the rectification of the people's virtue, attention to tools and conveniences, and ensuring abundance of life's necessities... When these nine services have been put in order, celebrate with song. Admonish the people with gentleness, correct them with authority, exhort them with the Nine Songs, and your reign will not diminish.' ❞

From the *Shu Jing*, translated by Jennifer Oldstone-Moore.

❝ Mengzi said, 'The compass and the square form perfect circles and squares; the sage brings about the perfect person. If one desires to become a ruler, one must carry out completely the role of the ruler; if one desires to become a minister, one must carry out completely the role of the minister. For these two, one need only follow the examples of Yao and Shun. Not to follow the example of Shun serving Yao is to disrespect one's prince; not to follow Yao as the model for governing the people is to harm the people.' ❞

From the *Mengzi*, translated by Jennifer Oldstone-Moore.

Commentary

Classical Confucianism is generally less concerned with issues such as the creation of the cosmos than with the beginnings of civilization—the origins of which, according to Confucian belief, are to be found in the lives of the legendary "sage kings" of antiquity (see pp.44–5).

Traditional Chinese history begins in the twenty-fourth century BCE with the reign of Yao. Both he and his successor Shun (ca. 2255–ca. 2205 BCE) ruled by ritual and benevolence rather than military might. The loving care that was extended to the people by them is an early and powerful expression of the idea of a ruler who is essentially a father to his subjects. Statecraft, as described (opposite) to Shun by his exemplary minister Yu, is concerned with the people's material and moral welfare—both of which were persistent themes in East Asian theories of kingship.

Yao, Shun, and Yu were held up by later generations as model rulers and ministers, as evidenced in the passage from the *Mencius*. Their actions and judgments were analyzed to provide solutions to contemporary problems. In the nineteenth century, faced with serious challenges from the West, Chinese Confucian scholars drew upon the examples of Yao and Shun in formulating their arguments for change.

CHAPTER TWO

ASPECTS OF THE DIVINE

Confucian concepts of the divine take two main forms. On the one hand, concerns focus on ordering principles—on cosmic forces and concepts of ultimate reality, such as Heaven and the Great Ultimate—which are subjects of contemplation rather than worship. On the other hand, there is a wide range of deities and spiritual beings, which are venerated and placated at shrines and temples.

In Confucianism, the worlds of the living and of the deities and spirits are closely linked. Ancestors are deceased family members; ghosts are dangerous beings who are placated through offerings. Humans who live exemplary lives may become gods and be appointed to the celestial hierarchy after death. Gods are, in turn, petitioned by humans, whose offerings sustain and nourish them.

LEFT: A scholar listens intently to running water. Landscape paintings had moral, ethical, and cosmological significance: they reflected the eternal principle (li) *that orders all creation and the disposition of a single object.*

Confucian concepts of the divine focus on an accessible spirit world and awesome but remote cosmic forces. These ancient beliefs are evident in the first Chinese records, the Shang oracle bones (see pp.12–13). Shang rulers sacrificed to their ancestors and also venerated a supreme being, Shang Di, the "Lord on High." With his subsequent displacement by Tian, or "Heaven," the "Mandate of Heaven" (see p.13) became central to the Confucian theory of government. This belief revealed Heaven as an entity with a will, concerned about and responsive to the welfare of the people. Confucius himself clearly understood Heaven as being both a natural and a moral order and believed that one must strive to know Heaven's will.

Perceiving the nature of cosmic order became an important aspect of Confucianism from the tenth century onward. Neo-Confucians developed a cosmology based on *li*, an ordering principle that shapes *qi*, the vital matter that makes up all things (see pp.6–8). Although there is apparent diversity in creation, all things are united by the Great Ultimate, *Taiji (T'ai-chi)*, the ordering principle of the cosmos. Through contemplation and investigation, humans can experience unity with the holy cosmos. The Neo-Confucian method of self-cultivation included intensive scholarship, a reverent attitude and disciplined mind, and "quiet-sitting"—meditation for purifying and focusing the mind which can produce a profoundly transformative experience. These ideas and practices became part of Confucian orthodoxy throughout East Asia.

Of more immediate concern to most people, however, was the multitude of spirits who could harm or help humans. The spirit world includes ancestors and gods, who receive offerings and reciprocate by means of favors and blessings, and ghosts, who are the unhappy, unpropitiated dead. "Heaven" is the dwelling place of the gods and is envisioned as a vast bureaucracy. The officials of the celestial realm wear the same regalia as those in the imperial bureaucracy; they are approached and petitioned in the same way as human officials—because they are just as susceptible to bribes and favors. In short, the worlds of the living and the dead not only mirror but interpenetrate each other.

At the top of this bureaucracy is the Jade Emperor, the spiritual counterpart of the terrestrial emperor. He is the supreme judge and sovereign of Heaven, the overseer of the administrative hierarchy. Appropriately, the Jade Emperor is a distant figure and it is possible to communicate with him only through intermediaries, just as an average person could not directly petition the emperor.

The ceiling of the Temple of Heaven, Beijing. The square base and the round, vaulted ceiling symbolize Earth and Heaven. Here, the emperor would perform annual sacrificial rituals to call upon Heaven to guarantee the order of his realm.

The lowest official in the celestial bureaucracy is one's local tutelary god, Tudi Gong, the "God of the Earth." Every neighborhood or village has its own Tudi Gong, who is likened to a village policeman or magistrate. It is his job to keep the peace, to quell local ghosts who cause trouble, and to be aware of what goes on in the area. Villagers might report events such as births, deaths, and marriages, both to Tudi Gong and to the local (mortal) police station. Tudi Gong passes on any relevant happenings to his superior in the celestial hierarchy.

One of the primary ideals of Confucianism is to promote virtuous officials in the bureaucracy. This ideal also applies to the spirit world, and can be seen in the story of Mazu, a fisherman's daughter who became Empress of Heaven. Mazu lived a short but exemplary life, and exhibited extraordinary spiritual powers. After she died at age twenty-eight, her spirit was venerated by the local population, and boats began to carry an image of her for protection. After two centuries of popular veneration, local Confucian literati noticed the popularity of her cult and tales of her generosity and service to the people. They recommended that she be promoted, and by imperial command she rose through the ranks of the celestial hierarchy until she was designated Empress of Heaven (Tian Hou), and became a consort of the Jade Emperor. Today, Mazu continues to be one of the most popular deities in southern China and Taiwan. Her story illustrates the connection between the élite and popular traditions, and Confucianism's effectiveness in influencing political and social structures.

The *Western Inscription* by Zhang Zai (1020–1077)

❝ Heaven is my father and Earth is my mother, and even such a small creature as I finds an intimate place in their midst. Therefore that which fills the universe I regard as my body and that which directs the universe I consider as my nature. All people are my brothers and sisters, and all things are my companions. The great ruler (the emperor) is the eldest son of my parents (Heaven and Earth), and the great ministers are his stewards. Respect the aged—this is the way to treat them as elders should be treated. Show deep love toward the orphaned and the weak—this is the way to treat them as the young should be treated. ... Do nothing shameful in the recesses of your own house and thus bring no dishonor to [Heaven and Earth]. Preserve your mind and nourish your nature and thus (serve them) with untiring effort. ...Wealth, honor, blessing, and benefits are meant for the enrichment of my life, while poverty, humble station, and sorrow are meant to help me to fulfillment. In life I follow and serve (Heaven and Earth). In death I will be at peace. **❞**

From *A Source Book in Chinese Philosophy*, by Wing-tsit Chan. Princeton University Press: Princeton, 1963, pp.497–98. Note: (Parentheses) are in the translator's original; [square brackets] are author's addition.

Commentary

In the *Western Inscription*, the Neo-Confucian scholar Zhang Zai succinctly and poetically describes the fundamentally interrelated nature of the cosmos and evokes the holiness and completeness of the created order. The influential text (which the author inscribed on the western wall of his study) reflects the idea that there is a principle—*li*—that underlies all creation. This principle is manifest in the orderly pattern of nature, which in an eternal cycle unfolds in creation and eventually returns to its undifferentiated state.

The underlying principle to which Zhang Zai refers is the Great Ultimate, or *Taiji*, the basis for all growth and change. *Taiji* is manifest as *qi*, vital matter, which differentiates into the *yin* and *yang* polarities, and then into the "Five Phases" (see pp.8–9) and myriad creation. All things, spiritual and physical, are made of *qi*, and thus all things are related: the universe is one. The text uses the evocative Confucian language of family relationships to articulate the relationship between all things in a cosmos in which there is no creator standing apart from creation. The sage strives to perceive the unity of the universe, comprehend its pattern, and harmonize with it.

CHAPTER THREE

SACRED TEXTS

In many religions, sacred texts are considered to be "divinely revealed"—the Confucian canon, however, is almost exclusively attributed to human beings. It includes the works of founding figures such as Confucius and Mencius, and covers subjects ranging from the origins of civilization and good government to the history and protocol of early dynasties.

The dominance of the Confucian canon in early East Asian civilizations was equal to that of the Bible in the West. In China, its texts were the source for moral and intellectual development, and they were the means by which the Chinese élite culture was transmitted to other East Asian civilizations. Although the canon no longer has the prominence it once did, the ideals that it promotes still have tremendous power in East Asian culture.

LEFT: An early 18th-century Chinese painting depicting the examination of county magistrates. Entry into this important stratum of the government bureaucracy was through open civil service tests, which would have required considerable knowledge of the Confucian Classics.

At the heart of the Confucian tradition are its scriptures, especially the "Five Classics" and the "Four Books." The Five Classics were revered in ancient China and, by the time of the Han dynasty, constituted the core of Confucian learning in Vietnam and Korea as well as in China. They were memorized by every aspiring student, formed the basis of civil service examinations, and were quoted not only by scholars and philosophers but also by bureaucrats. In Japan, the Five Classics were an important part of the borrowed heritage of China. In Korea and Vietnam, due to early Chinese political control, they formed the basis of élite culture.

Confucius saw himself as a mediator of the wisdom of the "sage kings" of antiquity (see pp.44–5). For him, this wisdom was accessible primarily through the study of the Classics: the *Classic of Changes* (*Yi Jing*, also *I Ching*), the *Classic of Documents* (*Shu Jing*), the *Classic of Poetry* (*Shi Jing*), the *Record of Rites* (*Li Ji*), and the *Spring and Autumn Annals* (*Chunqiu*). A sixth text, the *Classic of Music* (*Yue Jing*), was lost before the third century BCE.

Each of the Classics captures an important component of wisdom, promotes harmony and order, and provides the means to self-cultivation and becoming fully human. The *Classic of Changes* captures the tremendous importance of the ancient practice and theory of divination; it also underscores the intimate connection between the human and natural realm, and the availability of guidance from the cosmos for those who are sensitive to it. Attributed to the mythic emperor and culture-bearer Fu Xi, the *Classic of Changes'* system of divination is based on sixty-four hexagrams representing various combinations of *yin* and *yang* (see pp.8–9). These hexagrams are taken to represent all possible situations and developments in the constantly changing universe. Confucius is traditionally credited with writing the "Ten Wings', commentaries and expositions which help to decipher the abstruse, opaque judgments of the text.

The *Classic of Documents* is a record of historical events, some traditionally dated to China's remote past (third millennium BCE), providing lessons in moral behavior and good government. The *Spring and Autumn Annals* records events in the Zhou dynasty and has also been read for moral judgments and guidance for rulers. Both texts articulate the Confucian emphasis on looking to the past for direction and guidance.

The *Classic of Poetry* is a collection of 305 poems ranging from courtly airs to folk songs. One tradition has it that the Zhou kings collected the poems to assess the mood and concerns of the people—knowledge vital to a ruler who wishes to keep the Mandate of Heaven (see p.13). Many of the poems are read as allegorical commentaries on government. The *Record of Rites* is a collection of material that incorporates mundane house-hold instructions for the young, protocol for royalty, and philosophy. It articulates the template for the transfor-mative *li*—ritual, etiquette, and propriety—which is the basis of Confucian self-cultivation (see pp.54–5).

Traditionally, Confucius is credited with writing the *Spring and Autumn Annals* as well as the "Ten Wings," and with editing the four other classic texts. Modern scholarship holds that these texts were compiled throughout the Zhou dynasty, and the received texts are the result of recension in the Han following the Qin dynasty's practice of book burning (see p.15).

The Five Classics were augmented by other texts through the centuries, with a total of thirteen identi-fied by the ninth century CE. Song philosopher Zhu Xi brought together the "Four Books," asserting that they summed up the teachings of Confucius. They became the core texts of Confucian teaching in China from 1313 to 1905, with Zhu's commentary considered orthodoxy. The Four Books consist of the *Analects* (*Lunyu*) of Con-fucius, the *Mencius* (*Mengzi*), the *Great Learning* (*Daxue*) and the *Doctrine of the Mean* (*Zhongyong*).

The *Analects*, which formed part of the canon from

the Han dynasty onward, is a record of Confucius' own prescriptions for an ideal society recorded by his students. In it, he demonstrates how the rites (*li*) of early Chinese rulers provide a template for appropriate human interaction and methods of achieving virtuous government and a harmonious society. The *Mencius*, the works of Confucius' eponymous follower, expands on Confucius' teachings in the *Analects*. In this text, Mencius developed a theory of human beings as fundamentally good and educable—it is a theory that has had tremendous influence in the Confucian world. Another innovation of the *Mencius* is its assertion that subjects have the right to overthrow a corrupt or tyrannical ruler.

The *Great Learning* and the *Doctrine of the Mean* were originally written as chapters in the *Record of Rites*, and were selected by Zhu Xi for their philosophical and metaphysical import. The *Great Learning* teaches that the first step in bringing the world into harmony is the cultivation of the individual. Self-cultivation has a ripple effect that will spread eventually to the family, locality, region, world, and cosmos. The *Doctrine of the Mean* asserts that cosmos and humanity form a unity through sincere effort.

All of the texts in the Confucian canon are written in the terse, refined language of classical, "adorned,"

*"Friendship with the
upright, the devoted and
the learned is profitable."*

*"Think of justice at the
sight of profit, and sacrifice
when faced with danger."*

*"If you do not consider
the future, you will be in
trouble when it comes near."*

*"If you find you make a
mistake, then you must not
be afraid of correcting it."*

"Harmony is the most valuable."

"Rule by moral force."

A selection of maxims from Confucius' work, the Analects,
which has been described as the most influential text ever.

Chinese—their complexity gave rise to a tradition of commentary aimed at elucidation and interpretation. Study of the canon required years of focused effort. Chinese children began learning to write Chinese characters as young as four years old and were aided by texts that presented Confucian teachings in the form of jingles for easy memorization. Once capable, students would learn their texts by rote, only later studying commentaries to assist in understanding. For scholars in Japan, Korea, and Vietnam, mastering the Classics and other books of the canon also involved mastering a foreign language.

The lessons contained within the classic texts were disseminated in a number of ways for those who were unable to read them. In China, community schools were established and simplified manuals were written to teach the essence of the canon to the unlettered. During the Qing dynasty, the *Sacred Edict*, which contained basic teachings of Confucian morality and virtue, was read and explained to the populace by imperial decree. Morality tracts that contained Confucian lessons were popular, and texts featuring exemplars of filial piety were widely read in both China and Korea. Some accomplished scholars, notably Zhu Xi in China and Kaibara Ekken in Japan, wrote texts and manuals expressly for the use and edification of the common person.

"North Wind" from the *Classic of Poetry*

" The north wind is so cold;

The snow falls so thick.

Be tender; love me

Take my hand and we will go together.

You're so timid and so slow—

We must hurry, hurry! **"**

" The north wind is so strong;

The snow whirls so fast.

Be tender; love me

Take my hand and we will return together.

You're so timid and so slow—

We must hurry, hurry! **"**

" Nothing so red as the fox,

Nothing blacker than the crow;

Be tender; love me

Take my hand and we will ride in the carriage together.

You're so timid and so slow—

We must hurry, hurry! **"**

From the *Shi Jing*, translated by Jennifer Oldstone-Moore.

Commentary

The *Classic of Poetry* (from which this poem is taken; see pp.35–6) has been pivotal in Chinese literature and culture. It has been used to gauge the mood of the people, and thus to guide the government; as a repository of hymns for official functions; and as part of the required canon for the civil service. The poems in the collection are said to date from the twelfth to the seventh century BCE and range from courtly airs to folk songs. Their subject matter also varies greatly and includes love, war, agriculture, sacrifice, and dynastic legends.

"North Wind" is from a series of folk songs in the volume that speaks of the joys and concerns of common people—many of the pieces being love songs. However, Confucian literature always has a moral gloss and this poem has traditionally been interpreted not so much as a love poem as an indictment of a cruel government, a warning against tyrannical rule, and an advocacy of righteous and beneficent leadership. According to this reading, the first two stanzas are metaphorical references to oppressive conditions; the fox and the crow who appear in the final stanza are intended as omens of evil. In stressing rule by virtue, Confucians warn that subjects will flee a tyrant and flock to the country of a just ruler—illustrated here by the speaker's insistence on a hurried departure.

CHAPTER FOUR

SACRED PERSONS

In the Confucian tradition, various historic, legendary, semilegendary, and mythical figures are recognized for their saintly or heroic acts. These exemplars brought culture, social institutions, and good government to China to establish its golden age of antiquity. It is to them that Confucius looked when shaping the tradition he received, and the lives of many of them are related in the "Five Classics" (see pp.34–6).

Other illustrious individuals lived well after the golden age. They ranged from outstanding scholars who dutifully transmitted the ideals that Confucius had espoused, to ordinary people who exhibited exceptional behavior. Finally, some worthies so distinguished themselves in the mortal realm that they continued to exert influence in the lives of ordinary people from the celestial realm.

LEFT: A 17th–18th-century woodblock print of King Wen, the "civilizing king" who was one of the founders of the Zhou dynasty. Here he is depicted watching children at play among lotus flowers.

In China there is a rich mythology of heroes and culture bearers (semi-mythical figures believed to have brought humanity the basics of civilization). The most noted of these are Fu Xi, Shen Nong, and Huang Di. Fu Xi is credited with domesticating animals and inventing nets for catching animals and fish. He established the art of divination by devising the hexagram system of the Eight Trigrams used in the *Classic of Changes* (see pp.34–5) and, with his consort Nuwa, invented marriage and the family. Shen Nong, the Divine Farmer, invented the plow and hoe and taught humanity the skills of agriculture. He discovered the rudiments of medicine and pharmacology by determining the therapeutic qualities of all plants. Huang Di, the Yellow Emperor (see illustration, p.10), invented warfare and defeated "barbarians" to secure what became the heart of the Chinese state.

Chinese tradition considers the period following the culture bearers as the golden age of antiquity, the time of the "sage kings," especially Shun, Yao and Yu who exemplify the dedication, intelligence, and virtue appropriate to a ruler. Shun and Yao were praised by Confucius as examples of perfect rulers. Yao determined that none of his sons—ten in number—were worthy to rule, and therefore searched for the most virtuous man in the kingdom to succeed him. His criterion of virtue was filial piety, which was demonstrated by Shun, who continued to serve his father and stepbrother without complaint, despite their attempts to harm and even murder him. Shun became king and later also bypassed his sons, handing the succession to Yu, the founder of the legendary Xia dynasty (2205–1766BCE).

The story of Yu exemplifies the Chinese view of the ideal state, which is characterized by beneficent government and just rulers who strive to bring about order and harmony between nature and humanity. Yu's worthiness was demonstrated in his ceaseless physical labor to protect the people from flooding, China's most frequent form of natural disaster. His dedication to this task was so great that for ten years he did not visit his own home, even when he passed by so closely that he could hear the cries of his young children.

A complement to the ideal ruler and much praised by Confucius, the duke of Zhou (died 1094BCE) has long served as a model of the exemplary public servant who did his duty to uphold order and his dynasty, but without seeking the throne for himself. The duke was the brother of King Wu, founder of the Zhou dynasty, and showed his sensitivity to familial and social obligations by being an exemplary younger brother, devoted son, and loyal minister. After Wu died, the duke acted as regent for Wu's young son for seven years, never attempting to usurp the throne, in spite of accusations—subsequently disproved—to the contrary. This heroic role model proved so enduring that "duke of Zhou" was a popular nickname for the respected Communist premier Zhou Enlai (1898–1976). Yao, Shun, Yu and the duke of Zhou served as models of rulers and ministers in East Asia for centuries.

The great sage, Confucius, is also revered in the tradition, and with him his illustrious followers. In China, temples venerating Confucius were first established in the Han dynasty, and the temple at Qufu, Confucius's home town, became a national shrine. The first Confucian temple was built in Qufu in 478BCE, although no official sacrifice was made to the sage himself until 195BCE, when the Han emperor Gaodi (r. 206–195) offered the "Great Sacrifice" (*daji*), including the offering of an ox, at the tomb of Confucius. Confucian temples, which by the late empire were found in every province of China, held memorial services for Confucius in the second and eighth months of the Chinese lunar year. The Confucian temples honored Confucius and his most esteemed followers, some contemporaries of Confucius, and other later figures such as Mencius and Zhu Xi. The temples contained the memorial tablets of a

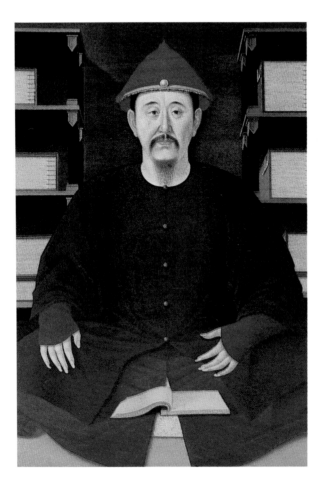

China's Emperor Kangxi (1662–1723) was a patron of Neo-Confucian learning and his practical system of dykes rivaled the work of the sage king Yu, the "Flood-tamer."

number of illustrious Confucians, carefully arranged according to rank and seniority. Confucius himself continued to be honored by state sponsored and mandated sacrifices throughout Chinese history. However, his status as a human and not a god was resolutely maintained, despite the not unusual practice of apotheosizing human heroes into the celestial bureaucracy. Today, his birthday is celebrated in a solemn and ancient ceremony at the Memorial Hall in Qufu and also at the Confucian temple in Taipei, where he is remembered as the First Teacher.

Confucian ideals were also the basis for recognizing contemporary worthies. In every dynasty there were heroes and heroines who embodied such ideals as the filial child, the chaste and devoted wife, and the virtuous and selfless public servant. In Korea and China their stories are recounted in texts such as the *Classic of Filial Piety*, the *Biographies of Heroic Women*, and the *Record of Filial Behavior*. Such stories include that of Laizi, who pretended to be a child even when he was more than seventy, so that his aged parents would not feel old; others tell of girls who committed suicide at the death of their fiancés in order to be loyal to their betrothed, and of the secondary wife who ran into a burning house to rescue the children of her husband's primary wife, leaving her own to perish.

Confucian ideals are also evident in the pantheon of Chinese popular religion. Even today, the pantheon is structured to parallel the Chinese imperial Confucian government—a celestial bureaucracy which complements the earthly bureaucracy below. Members of the hierarchy may be identified as being Daoist, Buddhist, or some other designation, but all are subject to the same expectations of an official in the bureaucracy, patterned on stereotypes of Confucian bureaucrats. Confucian statecraft holds that those who exhibit virtue such as filiality, loyalty, righteousness, and selflessness should be promoted. Likewise, deities in the imperial pantheon could be promoted, often by (terrestrial) imperial decree, through the ranks of the celestial hierarchy. Perhaps the most famous example of this is the widely popular Guan Di, a military hero of the Han era (206BCE–220CE). Throughout the centuries, he was promoted by imperial decree through the ranks of the celestial hierarchy, and continues today to be the patron god of many trades and professions. The apotheosis of Guan Di and other figures in the Chinese pantheon demonstrates the pervasive influence of Confucian ideas and structures in the popular imagination, and the syncretic nature of the popular religion, which incorporates Confucian ideals seamlessly with those of other traditions.

Selections from the *Analects* of Confucius

❝ 2:4 Confucius said, 'At fifteen it was my desire to learn. At thirty I was established. At forty I had no more doubts. At fifty I knew Heaven's will. At sixty I could obey what I heard. At seventy I could follow my heart's desire and not transgress what is right.' **❞**

❝ 5:25 Zilu said, 'I would like to hear your ideals.' Confucius said, 'My ideals are to bring solace to the old, to be faithful to friends, and to cherish the young.' **❞**

❝ 7:7 Confucius said, 'Upon receiving as little as a few pieces of dried meat for tuition, I have not yet refused to teach a person.' **❞**

❝ 7:18 The Duke of She asked Zilu about Confucius and Zilu did not answer. Confucius said, 'Why didn't you say that I am a person who studies with such eagerness that he forgets his food, is so happy that he forgets his cares, and does not notice the coming of old age?' **❞**

❝ 7:19 Confucius said, 'I am not one who was born with knowledge; I am one who loves antiquity and diligently seeks knowledge there.' **❞**

From the *Analects* (*Lunyu*) of Confucius, translated by Jennifer Oldstone-Moore.

Commentary

Confucius, or Kong Qiu (known in China as Kongzi or Master Kong), was born in 552BCE in the state of Lu, which is in modern-day Shandong province. It is thought that he was descended from nobility, perhaps even the Shang royal family; however, his own family was humble and he was orphaned as a child. He died in 479BCE, age 73. His most significant contribution was as an educator rather than as a government official, and he is still celebrated as the first and greatest teacher in much of East Asia.

The most reliable source of information about Confucius is the *Analects* (*Lunyu*), the recorded conversations between him and his disciples. In this text, he is revealed as one who loved learning and culture, observed the details of ritual with sincere earnestness rather than pompous formalism, and was committed and attentive to others, especially his disciples (Zilu, mentioned in the extract opposite, was one of his favorite students). Although most of his teachings focused on the human realm, it is clear that he perceived his civilizing mission as coming from Heaven, which protected and inspired him. Confucius has perhaps been the single most important figure in East Asian culture—his teachings remain influential in the present day.

CHAPTER FIVE

ETHICAL PRINCIPLES

Confucian ethics, which have served as the basis of East Asian society for at least 2,000 years, are directed toward the creation of a harmonious society and a virtuous, benevolent state. It is believed that these ideals can be achieved through the practice of *li* (ritual and protocol) and *ren* (humaneness).

Confucianism demands that all people be treated with humanity, but within a well-articulated hierarchy. Filial piety is a central Confucian virtue, as is behaving according to one's rank. The most important relationships are those between parent and child, husband and wife, elder brother and younger brother, friend and friend, ruler and subject. An ordered, harmonious society is dependent on self-education and on each person playing his or her part appropriately and with good intent.

LEFT: A 19th-century print of a Chinese wedding ceremony shows the bride and groom kneeling before a tablet honoring "Heaven, Earth, parents, and teachers." The husband-and-wife family unit was central to the transmission of Confucian values in society.

Confucians hold that actions are transformative—to become an ethical person, one must be self-cultivated through the study and practice of appropriate behavior. At the heart of Confucian ethics is the *li*, the "guiding principle of all things great and small" (*Analects* 1:12), which is held to be the behavior of the sages of antiquity as recorded in the classic texts. *Li* has a range of meanings: ritual, propriety, etiquette, and ceremony; it denotes ideal behavior, and moral and righteous action, and is the means by which one works to "cut, carve, file and polish," in order to become a superior person and cultivate ethical behavior.

Other forms of cultivation also contribute to ethical development. Refinement in the arts, or *wen*, follows the example of the sages who created poetry, music, and ritual. According to Confucius, those who study literature extensively and who are restrained by the *li*, are truly superior, and will not violate the "Confucian Way." Thus, Confucians strive to master the fine arts—such refinement is the mark not only of aesthetic taste, but also of moral training.

The *li* provides a template for appropriate action which, once internalized, is expressed in human interaction. The actions of the self-cultivated person are *ren*, the ethical term referred to most frequently by Confucius in the *Analects*. *Ren* is defined as goodness, humane-ness, love, benevolence, human-heartedness, and humanity. The word is rendered with two component parts that denote "person" and "two," indicating the relationship between two people. Together *li* and *ren* form the basis of ethical behavior which is balanced between self-cultivation and learning and the effortless extension of learning into human interaction.

Action in accordance with *ren* is manifest in attitude and external expression in two other virtues—reciproc-ity (*shu*) and sincerity (*zhong*). Reciprocity forms the basis of the Confucian golden rule—"What you do not want done to you, do not do to others" (*Analects* 15:23). Rather than assuming that others will like what one likes, one must consider actions from the other person's point of view. The ethic of *zhong* provides a basis for the action of reciprocity—sincerity is a feeling, an internal orientation, that manifests itself in proper action.

All interaction must be based in *ren*, but specific actions are delineated within a clearly defined hierarchy (hierarchy is considered to be natural and essential to the creation of harmony). Key roles and corresponding virtues are outlined in the "Five Relationships," namely, those between parent and child, elder brother and younger brother, husband and wife, friend and friend, and ruler and subject. Each relationship has its specific roles and responsibilities: a parent owes a child education, care, and moral formation; a child owes a parent obedience, respect, and care in old age and after death. The parent/child relationship establishes the basic pattern for other relationships—thus, the virtue of filiality (*xiao*) is the basis for social structure. A husband and wife are to care for each other, with the husband protecting and providing, and the wife being obedient and maintaining the household. The elder brother has responsibility for younger siblings who owe him deference (birth order is very clearly delineated in East Asian kinship terms). The relationship between ruler and subject parallels that of parent and child, for the ruler is to provide care and guidance, and the subject is to be obedient as well as loyal. Friends are to be loyal—this is the only relationship that has the potential of being between people of equal rank, but even here, a hierarchy of age is often reflected.

Although obedience and deference are demanded from subordinates within this structure of relationships, a good son, worthy wife, and loyal minister have a duty to remonstrate unethical behavior. All five relationships (as well as others, such as those between teacher and student, and employer and employee) have serious mutual responsibilities, and both familial and non-familial bonds are presumed to last a lifetime. Ethical action includes the "rectification of names," which means knowing one's roles in the web of relationships that create community, and behaving accordingly so as to insure social harmony.

Confucian ethics are particularly important in the realm of government. The ruler as sovereign and father-figure is to be an active exemplar of virtue. "The ruler is to be like the wind; the people like the grass that bends in whatever direction the wind blows (*Analects* 12:19). Self-cultivation, a cultured education, and a life lived according to *li* were deemed essential for the aspiring government official. Such figures were urged to exhibit their firm principles by chastising the emperor himself if his rule was not virtuous and withdrawing from service rather than aiding a despot: "Show yourself when the Way prevails in the empire; when it does not, then hide" (*Analects* 8:13). After the Mongols invaded China and founded the Yuan dynasty in 1279, many courtiers chose "virtuous retirement" in preference to serving the "barbarian" foreign ruler.

Confidence in the universality of Confucian ethics was challenged in the nineteenth and twentieth centuries as a consequence of the influence of Western ideas and technology. Many hoped that Confucianism would continue to provide the ethical basis of East Asian life; others saw it as the root of East Asian weakness and called for a complete dismantling of the systems and ideas of which Confucianism was a central part. Some hoped that its values could be combined with Western technology, or, as it was stated in China, "Chinese studies for substance; Western studies for function."

This hope has been repeatedly reformulated and revisited throughout East Asia in the last 100 years. The new Chinese republic drafted a constitution in 1913 that advocated Confucianism as the basis of moral cultivation and education; Chiang Kai-shek attempted to impress Confucian values on the populace of the Republic of China through various programs and proclamations; today, groups in Taiwan and Korea advocate Confucian teachings and a return to "traditional values." The city-state of Singapore is especially notable for its systematic program of Confucian ethics in the schools, which was promoted by the government in the 1980s. The cardinal principles of this program show the Confucian emphasis on harmony and working to the good of the group. They teach the importance of considering community over self, affirm the family as the basic unit of society, and emphasize the necessity for tolerance and

A 16th-century ceramic box lid depicts a district magistrate trying a case. As the local representatives of the imperial government, magistrates were steeped in Confucian learning.

harmony in a religiously and ethnically diverse society. These programs have been instigated and supported by top officials in Singapore to strengthen Asian cultural heritage and to protect the region from the venality and excess of Western culture, demonstrating both continuity and change in classical Confucian ethics.

Daxue (the *Great Learning*)

" . . . Things have their roots and their branches ... their conclusions and beginnings. When one knows what comes first and what comes last, one will come near the Way. Those of old who wished to manifest clear virtue to all the world first governed their states; those who wished to govern their states first set their families in order; those who wished to set their families in order first cultivated their persons; those who wished to cultivate their persons first rectified their own hearts and minds; those who wished to rectify their own hearts and minds first made their thoughts sincere; those who wished to make their thoughts sincere first extended their knowledge. Extension of knowledge rests in the investigation of things.

When things are investigated, knowledge is extended; when knowledge is extended, thoughts are made sincere; when thoughts are made sincere, the heart and mind are rectified; when the heart and mind are rectified, one's person is cultivated; when one's person is cultivated, the family is set in order; when the family is set in order, the state is governed; when the state is governed, there is peace in all the world. "

From the *Daxue*, translated by Jennifer Oldstone-Moore.

Commentary

The *Great Learning*, or *Daxue*, which also means "adult education," was originally a chapter in the *Record of Rites* (one of the "Five Classics"). It was among the texts selected by the Neo-Confucian philosopher Zhu Xi in his compilation of the "Four Books" (see pp.34–7), and was one of the first texts learned by all students. With its focus on self-cultivation, education, and bringing order to the world, the *Great Learning* sums up the Confucian program for balancing development of the self with responsibility to others. It is a work that has had a profound influence on Confucian ethics, practice, and philosophy.

The Confucian program for transformation is accomplished in eight stages that have been described as a blueprint for putting the ethical principle of *ren* (humaneness, see pp.54–5) into practice. Transformation through *ren* begins with the self and leads ultimately to the pacification of "All under Heaven." Vital to this process is the ability to discern "roots and ... branches," "conclusions and beginnings," and the "first and ... last." Perceiving the relative importance of things—such as knowing one's specific obligations, which range from courtesy to a stranger to obedience to parents—is understood to be at the heart of this endeavour.

Commentary

The *Great Learning*, or *Daxue*, which also means "adult education," was originally a chapter in the *Record of Rites* (one of the "Five Classics"). It was among the texts selected by the Neo-Confucian philosopher Zhu Xi in his compilation of the "Four Books" (see pp.34–7), and was one of the first texts learned by all students. With its focus on self-cultivation, education, and bringing order to the world, the *Great Learning* sums up the Confucian program for balancing development of the self with responsibility to others. It is a work that has had a profound influence on Confucian ethics, practice, and philosophy.

The Confucian program for transformation is accomplished in eight stages that have been described as a blueprint for putting the ethical principle of *ren* (humaneness, see pp.54–5) into practice. Transformation through *ren* begins with the self and leads ultimately to the pacification of "All under Heaven." Vital to this process is the ability to discern "roots and ... branches," "conclusions and beginnings," and the "first and ... last." Perceiving the relative importance of things—such as knowing one's specific obligations, which range from courtesy to a stranger to obedience to parents—is understood to be at the heart of this endeavour.

CHAPTER SIX

SACRED SPACE

In Confucianism there is frequently no clear distinction between the sacred and the profane—the sacred may be encountered in nature and in the world at large, as well as in temples, shrines, and the home. Space that is specifically designated as sacred is primarily ritual space, and ranges from simple sites where small offerings are made, to grand imperial spaces where complex rites are conducted.

Since the end of the traditional Confucian state, many temples have decayed or declined in use. However, some have been restored and maintained and, in 1988, amid lavish celebrations, a new Confucian temple was opened in Andong county in Korea—ceremonies were performed to install the ritual tablets of eighteen Chinese disciples and eighteen Korean scholars of Confucianism.

LEFT: The Jade Bridge at the Temple of Confucius in Qufu, in Shandong province. First built in 478BCE, and much expanded since, the complex has hundreds of buildings, including Confucius' tomb in the Kong family cemetery.

Confucian temples are monuments to human beings rather than to gods and serve to honor Confucius and his disciples, as well as worthy scholars through the ages. The human orientation of the temples is further emphasized by the general lack of images and statues—instead, Confucius' name, as well as the names of his disciples and illustrious followers, are inscribed on tablets which act as the focus of veneration.

Members of the state bureaucracy traditionally honored Confucius in twice-yearly sacrifices on the equinoxes. The most important offering was on Confucius' birthday, which is still celebrated at Confucian temples. The event generally falls on September 28 and is celebrated as "Teacher's Day" in Taiwan. Participants dress in the garb of ancient China, perform dance and music, and offer sacrifices to the great sage.

Confucian temple architecture echoes the architecture of the emperor's palace—notably, the north–south axis on which the important halls are located. The temples are built on a square base, and internally they are symmetrical, with each wall a mirror-image of the one opposite, conveying the order associated with Confucian thought. Temples were public spaces—results of civil service examinations were posted in them and they were also used for training in music and ritual.

The first Confucian temple was built in Qufu in Shandong province in 478 BCE, the year after Confucius' death. Official sacrifices to Confucius began in 195 BCE, when the Han emperor offered a Grand Sacrifice at Qufu; the Han later adopted Confucianism as the basis of the state cult. Adjacent to the temple is the Kong family mansion, the home of the direct descendants of Confucius from the first century BCE, when the Han government granted the family a fiefdom and title. Later dynasties also supported the temple and the family with grants of land and imperial funds. The Confucian temple and the family mansion have defined and, through the extent of their landholdings, dominated Qufu. Beginning in the Ming dynasty, the district magistrate's office was located within the mansion compound; the only other residence also to serve as a government office was the imperial palace.

Other places of import for the Confucian tradition are schools and academies. These were centers for moral formation, places that provided the means and context to experience the ultimate as prescribed by Zhu Xi's "investigation of things", constituted communities for Confucian scholars, and were the locus for many rituals honoring the Great Sage. Schools supported by the state were established in Korea, China, and Vietnam. In China, although the wealthiest had the easiest access to

An annual ritual in honor of Confucius being conducted at the Munmyo shrine in Seoul, the heart of Korean Confucianism.

education, most dynasties sought to make education available to exceptional students regardless of background or ability to pay. Schools were staffed by men who had received a classical Confucian education or had passed but not taken up a government appointment. In premodern East Asia, numerous academies in China and Korea were places of advanced learning where scholars and their disciples gathered to discuss Confucian thought, and to compile, preserve, and, in the last several centuries, publish texts. Scholars attached to an academy might be assigned a room and a stipend. Some academies still exist today: Korea's Seongkyunkwan University, which was the center of Confucian studies in Seoul, continues to perform rites for Confucians twice yearly, and still, theoretically, controls the local Confucian schools, of which there are more than 200.

South of the emperor's palace in Beijing is a large sacred complex that was one of the holiest sites of imperial China: the Temple of Heaven. Here, the emperor would perform rituals such as the annual sacrifices on the winter solstice when *yin* energy was at its peak and *yang*, bringing growth, warmth, and light, was just beginning to reemerge. As the Son of Heaven, the sole intermediary between Heaven (Tian) and the empire (Tian Xia, "All under Heaven"), he alone could perform such sacrifices. Through his sacrifices, the emperor of China played his part to guarantee cosmic order.

The Temple of Heaven was sacred ground—commoners were not allowed even to watch the silent procession of the emperor and his entourage from the imperial palace to the temple. On the winter solstice, the emperor offered incense, jade, silk, and wine. He sacrificed a red bullock, symbolizing *yang*, and prostrated himself nine times (nine is considered the most *yang* of numbers) before the altar to Heaven.

For most people, however, the family altar and the ancestral shrine are the most significant places of sacred activity. The home itself is the basic unit of Confucian practice—it is here that important relationships are played out, and where individuals receive the training that will shape them into virtuous members of the family and society. The altar—where gods and spirits as well as family ancestors may reside—is usually in the main living space of the house. Manuals outlining procedures for ritual carefully delineate correct placement of spirit tablets, which house ancestors. The tablets include the names of individual ancestors and birth and death dates, and often the number of sons. When three to five generations have passed, tablets are taken to the ancestral shrine where they receive regular sacrifices which are conducted by the extended family.

Confucianism affirms the sacrality of the universe. Human destiny, which is realized through fulfilment of one's social roles, is as much a part of cosmic order as any aspect of nature. Human virtues are evident in the patterns of creation, such as the regularity of the nodes on bamboo, which is associated with human constancy. Certain features of the landscape—for example, rivers, caves, and mountains—are believed to possess spiritual power. In China, Taishan (Mount Tai), the most important of five sacred mountains, was seen as a provider of fertility, a preventer of natural disasters, and a symbol of stability. It was worshiped as part of the folk tradition in spring and fall to ensure a successful planting and an abundant harvest. It was also the site of the rare *feng* and *shan* sacrifices. These rituals, addressed to Heaven and Earth, were performed by emperors to mark the founding of a new dynasty or the achievements of the emperor who requested favor for the dynasty from Heaven and Earth.

According to Confucian thought, the links between Heaven and humankind, and the responsiveness of Heaven to human affairs, were manifest in nature. The emperor's mandate to govern and his fulfilment of ritual duties and continued virtuous rule were evident in the regular and predictable motion of heavenly bodies, the successful growth of crops, and the continuation of order in the empire. If Heaven was not satisfied with the emperor, the harmony and regular rhythms of the natural and human worlds would be disrupted. Portents of chaos, such as floods, earthquakes, famine, drought, and uprisings, indicated Heaven's displeasure—and if they continued, they could ultimately legitimate the replacement of the dynasty.

The National Academy

66 At daybreak each morning, with the beating of a
drum, the headmaster along with the instructors of the
academy assemble the students in the courtyard ... the
students enter the hall where lectures and discussions on
the Classics take place. They study, deliberate, counsel,
and assist one another to reach a full understanding of
the relationships between ruler and minister, father and
son, husband and wife, elder brother and younger
brother, and friend and friend. For days and months,
together they work and rest as one body to train themselves ... It is from these students that the future loyal
ministers and the future filial sons are produced in
prolific number to serve the state and their families. [...]
Some people object that since the sage's teachings are
many, there is no reason why this hall alone should be
called the Hall of Illustrating the Cardinal Principles.
To them I say: The relationships between ruler and
minister, father and son, husband and wife, elder
brother and younger brother, and friend and friend are
rooted in the heavenly principle, and hence they are
unchanging and everlasting. How can there be any
teaching more important than this? 99

From *Sinjŭng Tongguk yŏji sŭngnam*, translated by Yongho Ch'oe, cited in *Sourcebook of Korean Civilization*, Vol. 1, edited by Peter H. Lee. Columbia University Press: New York, 1993, pp.523–24.

Commentary

Two persistent characteristics of the Confucian tradition, both of which are evident in the source quoted here, are its sense of the sacredness of everyday existence and the penetration of its ethical teachings into all aspects of East Asian culture and society. The intellectual emphasis of the teaching of Korea's sixteenth-century National Academy was the same as that of the Confucian "sage kings" of antiquity (see pp.44–5)—that is, the "Five Relationships" were considered to be the basis of all moral and intellectual development. Teachers were required to be stern taskmasters and disciplinarians, for it was believed that the fate of society and the state was in their hands.

The Neo-Confucian scholar Zhu Xi (1130–1200CE) held that since all human beings share the same nature, all should receive appropriate education. To that end, there was a proliferation of schools and academies, both privately and government-funded, ranging from national universities to humble regional schools. During the Choson, or Yi, period (1392–1910), Korea had an exemplary educational system—to such an extent that court officials would offer "royal lectures" to the ruler, reflecting the Confucian ideal that it is an enlightened and cultured monarch who can best serve the people.

CHAPTER SEVEN

SACRED TIME

There is great regional variety in East Asian observances of sacred time. The Confucian emphasis on family and society is a common theme linking the diverse celebrations of China, Korea, Japan, and Vietnam, which can simultaneously express various ideals, including those of Buddhism, Daoism, Shinto, and local religious practices. Confucianism has always been influential in shaping the region's celebrations, and historically, the Chinese calendar has included the observances of the state cult which were formally linked with the Confucian tradition.

In the Confucian world, success and good fortune are contingent upon a person's ability to align his or her actions with cosmic forces—discerning and responding to temporal patterns are therefore essential to auspicious behavior and the timely fulfillment of obligations.

*LEFT:
Offerings of incense are made in honor of the dead at the Qingming festival, which follows two weeks after the spring equinox. The festival focuses on uniting family members and renewing ties with the dead.*

In China, time is reckoned using a complex system combining solar and lunar calendars. Underlying this system is the ancient *yin-yang* cosmology (see pp.8–9), manifest in the waxing (*yang*) and waning (*yin*) phases of the moon and the seasonal round of growth and decay in the agricultural year. The lunar calendar consists of twelve months, with intercalary months added every two or three years. The solar year is divided into twenty-four periods of approximately fifteen days, called "nodes," or "breaths." The "breaths" reflect the patterns of climatic and celestial change through the year: eight are named after the equinoxes, solstices, and starts of seasons; others evoke agriculturally and meteorologically significant phenomena and have names such as "Insects Awaken" (early March); "Limit of Heat" (late August); and "Frost Descends" (late October).

The years are organized into a twelve-year cycle represented by the animals of the Chinese zodiac. This in turn is part of a sixty-year cycle which employs the zodiac animals, the "Five Colors" (blue, red, yellow, white, and black), and two sets of symbols, the "Ten Heavenly Stems" and "Twelve Earthly Branches." Each animal is associated with one Branch, and each color correlates to two Stems. Thus, 2000 was the year of the White Dragon; 2012 will be the year of the Black

Dragon. The first year of the sixty-year cycle is *jiazi*, the year of the Blue Rat (most recently, 1984).

Within the year, there are a number of widely observed celebrations. It would be inaccurate to designate these as strictly Confucian; rather, Confucian ideals —such as the desire for children, family togetherness, and harmony—permeate the actions and sentiments of the festivals. These themes are combined with objectives identified with other religious traditions, such as the pursuit of longevity, salvation from Hell, and protection from malevolent forces.

The most important holiday of the Chinese calendar, and one celebrated throughout East Asia, is the Lunar New Year or Spring Festival, celebrated to mark the return of the creative forces of *yang* after the peak of *yin* at the winter solstice. The festival begins on the first day of the first lunar month, usually between January 21st and February 19th. All family members return home, debts are paid, and quarrels settled. Seasonal foods are prepared, and the house is thoroughly cleansed of the old year's dirt and "inauspicious breaths," and decorated with the lucky color red and auspicious words and symbols. On New Year's Eve, the entire family gathers for a feast. The table is set to include dead family members, who are present in spirit. Having sealed

the door against evil spirits, the family talks and plays
games through the night, carefully avoiding unlucky or
negative topics and words. The seal of the door is broken
at the moment of the New Year to welcome the first

*During an annual visit to the tomb of Fu Xi, China's great
ancestral figure, villagers offer a prayer at a hexagram, the
original of which he was said to have discovered in antiquity.*

breath of spring. For the first two days of the year no one is to work, and there are prohibitions on sweeping or using blades for fear of "brushing away" or "cutting off" the good luck of the New Year. The final night of the two-week festival is the Lantern Festival, the first full moon of the New Year. Crowds gather amid beautiful displays of lanterns to watch stiltwalkers, lion dancers, and people in traditional costumes.

The Clear and Bright festival (Qingming) follows two weeks after the spring equinox. Ideally, the entire family gathers at Qingming to tend the family gravesite and share a picnic. The offerings include the deceased's favorite foods, and "saluting the tomb rice" and "longevity noodles" which symbolize blessings conferred by the ancestors and the hopes of the family. These offerings are presented with eating utensils and condiments, as one would serve food to any family member. Once the ancestors have consumed the "spiritual essence" of the food, the living family members consume the remainder. Qingming is a means of demonstrating family unity to outsiders while at the same time ritually remembering the dead and reinforcing family bonds.

Other widely celebrated holidays are the Double Fifth, Hungry Ghost, and Mid-Autumn festivals. The Double Fifth falls on the fifth day of the fifth lunar month, close to the summer solstice, when *yang* forces are at their annual peak. Traditionally the season of epidemics, this is a time to avert danger to the family through the use of prophylactic herbs and grasses which are hung on front doors, and the symbolism of the "Five Poisons" (centipede, snake, scorpion, toad, and lizard), which repel danger with their power. This is also the season of heavy rains and transplanting rice seedlings into paddies. Traditionally, the water was linked to dragons who bless the Earth with fertility.

The famous "dragon boat" races that take place on the Double Fifth reflect this lore as well as the legend of Zhou dynasty poet and dedicated minister Qu Yuan. After giving unpopular advice he was sent into exile, where he composed his most famous poem, *Li Sao* ("Encountering Sorrow"). Brokenhearted, he threw himself into the Miluo river in present-day Hunan province. People raced out in boats but failed to save him; they threw rice into the water so that the fish would eat the grain instead of Qu Yuan's body. Tradition has it that dragon boat races reenact the frantic search for Qu Yuan. The rice thrown to the fish is represented today by *zongzi*, sticky rice dumplings wrapped in bamboo leaves.

Like Qingming, the spirits of the deceased are central to the Hungry Ghost Festival, which falls on the fifteenth day of the seventh month. This festival is markedly different from Qingming, however, in that those propitiated are the dispossessed dead rather than beloved family members. Popular lore has it that the gates of Hell are opened during the seventh month; ghosts must be propitiated with offerings of food to avert danger and they are exhorted in formal Buddhist and Daoist ceremonies to turn from their evil ways. Comparing the food offerings given to ancestors and ghosts is instructive: ghosts are fed "at the back door" and given coarse foods that require little preparation. Ancestors, on the other hand, are offered carefully prepared dishes. They are honored members of the family who are tended at their burial sites and in the home.

The Mid-Autumn festival falls at full moon, the fifteenth day of the eighth lunar month. A harvest festival and a time for family gathering, it also celebrates the moon and the quest for immortality. In Chinese myth, the moon is home to a rabbit that pounds special herbs to make the elixir of immortality, and to the moon goddess, Chang E. A table is set up outdoors and laden with "moon cakes" and round, moon-shaped fruit such as oranges and melons. Families gather to watch the harvest moon and they recite stories and poems on lunar themes.

Chinese religious celebrations focus on family and community rather than the individual. Other than death, when a person becomes an ancestor, the most significant Chinese rite of passage is marriage, which assures the continuation of the family through the promise of descendants. Traditionally, a marriage became official when the couple bowed before the ancestral tablets of the groom, introducing the bride to her husband's forebears. Such practices maintain the link between the living and the dead, represent proper filial behavior, and ensure the blessings of the ancestors on the family. There were also coming of age ceremonies for boys and girls, but these were not of primary importance, and over time they came to be celebrated just before marriage rather than at a particular age. The sixtieth birthday is significant, however, for it symbolizes the completion of the cycle of years.

The observances that could most appropriately be deemed "Confucian" were those of the state cult which were performed by the emperor and his designated representatives, the scholar-officials. These solemn rituals had their roots in Chinese antiquity and showed the confluence of the ideals of filial behavior and virtuous, Heaven-mandated government. In the imperial capital, the emperor made offerings to the great celestial and earthly forces. Worship of Heaven and Earth at the winter and summer solstices respectively was particularly significant. The emperor was the pivot between Heaven, Earth, and humanity and his timely sacrifices ensured that cosmos and humanity remained in proper balance. As the symbolic son of Heaven and Earth, the emperor would kneel and prostrate himself to these powers as an act of filiality and on behalf of all the people of the state. At Qingming the emperor ensured the proper relation to imperial forebears and exemplars through his sacrifice to his own ancestors, to those of all past emperors, and to the culture heroes of antiquity. Finally, he sanctioned the semi-annual sacrifices made to Confucius on his behalf.

The emperor alone had the privilege and responsibility of worshiping these great cosmic forces—for anyone else to do so was considered an act of rebellion. Setting the calendar was also an imperial prerogative. Rites and festivals in the empire were carried out in accordance with an annual almanac of predicted celestial events issued by the official Bureau of Astronomy, a department of the Ministry of Rites. Imperial foreknowledge in such matters indicated harmony between the emperor and Heaven; any unexpected cosmic event could be interpreted as a sign of imminent loss of the sovereign's mandate to rule.

A Prayer to the Ruler on High, Shang Di

❝ 'Of old in the beginning, there was the great chaos, without form and dark. The five elements had not begun to revolve, nor the sun and the moon to shine. In the midst thereof there existed neither form nor sound. Thou, O spiritual Sovereign, camest forth in Thy presidency, and first didst divide the grosser parts from the purer. Thou madest heaven; Thou madest earth; Thou madest man. All things with their reproducing power, got their being....

'Thou hast vouchsafed, O Te [Shang Di], to hear us, for Thou regardest us as a Father. I, Thy child, dull and unenlightened, am unable to show forth my dutiful feelings. I thank Thee, that Thou has accepted the intimation. Honourable is Thy great name. With reverence we spread out these gems and silks, and, as swallows rejoicing in the spring, praise Thine abundant love. . . The meat has been boiled in the large caldrons, and the fragrant provisions have been prepared. Enjoy the offering, O Te, then shall all the people have happiness. I, Thy servant, receiving Thy favours, am blessed indeed.' **❞**

From *The Notions of the Chinese Concerning Gods and Spirits* by James Legge (his excerpt translation). Hong Kong, 1852, p. 28.

Commentary

According to the *yin-yang* cosmology of East Asia, time was cyclical rather than linear; the annual rites of the winter solstice at the Altar of Heaven ensured the continuation of proper temporal patterns. These were acts of the highest reverence, and the exalted nature of the high god Shang Di required that the emperor undergo extensive rites of purification. After extensive preparations, the elaborate rituals began before daylight on the winter solstice, with a large retinue, rich offerings, and humble prostrations.

Correct timing was crucial to these rites of renewal. Various departments of the Ministry of Rites painstakingly prepared a ritual calendar of sacred and lucky days (almanacs with this information are still used throughout East Asia to determine the appropriate times for various activities). The calendar was then issued to government offices and local magistrates, in order to guarantee timely performance of ritual duties. For the emperor's part, at the Altar of Heaven on the winter solstice, time and space would intersect in his person and actions, ensuring that the cosmic ebb and flow of *yin* and *yang* would continue smoothly and that the *yang* force of spring would return.

CHAPTER EIGHT

DEATH AND THE AFTERLIFE

East Asian attitudes toward death and the afterlife reflect ideas drawn from all the major regional traditions. Confucianism is not directly concerned with belief in an afterlife, although the Confucian virtue of filial piety is crucial to understanding the life of the dead and the responsibility of the living toward them. Several celebrated sayings by Confucius show his reluctance to speculate on the spirit world and his preference to focus on the responsibility of humans in this life.

However, in popular practice and belief, Confucian rites are part of a long history of communication with the spirit world. Here, ritual involves care for revered ancestors and the placation of ghosts—such rituals for the dead link the idealism and humanitarianism of the élite and the beliefs of the common people.

LEFT: A late 17th- or early 18th-century ancestor portrait. The Chinese have long believed that ancestors watch over and protect the living. Confucius emphasized the practice of ancestor worship, teaching that it could play an important role in insuring the continuity of the family.

Although it is difficult to speak of Confucian ideas of the afterlife independently of the other traditions that constitute East Asian religions, there are many ways in which Confucian beliefs have contributed to shaping the attitudes and practices of East Asians relating to death and the afterlife.

The rites of ancestor veneration, which are a significant reflection of attitudes toward death and the afterlife, have been a defining feature of East Asian civilizations for millennia. Concerns about the dead and communication with them date at least to the Chinese Shang dynasty (ca. 1766–1050BCE). The Shang presumed a close relationship between the living and the dead—ritual was highly significant in that it bridged the gap between the two realms. These rituals and sacrifices were codified in the Zhou dynasty (1050–256BCE), and were part of the *li* revered by Confucius.

Early Confucians outlined the obligations and appropriate behavior of children toward deceased forebears rather than described the fate of the dead or the nature of the afterlife. Confucius wished to create a righteous society, and saw rites for the dead as expressions of filial piety which revealed the depth and sincerity of love for forebears. Such rites would be performed by all people, regardless of rank and, like all *li*, had a transformative effect—they were thus of tremendous importance as it was believed that they were instrumental in creating a harmonious and ordered society.

Early Confucians assumed the existence of an after-life, but the few comments made by Confucius on the subject indicate a reluctance to discuss such matters. He spoke of respecting spiritual beings while at the same time keeping one's focus firmly on the human realm and on performing duties on behalf of humankind; he criticized as mere flatterers those who would make sacrifices to other people's ancestors. In one famous *Analects'* passage, he asked, "If we are not able to serve humanity, how can we serve spiritual beings?... If we do not understand life, how can we know about death?" (11:11). Such aloofness characterized the attitude of the élite toward a host of practices and beliefs that were part of the popular tradition—they focused instead on a legacy of virtuous example, service in government, and the study of scholarly works passed down through the ages.

But for the literati and the common people alike, rituals were of the utmost importance. The most basic are the daily rites at the family altar, which is in many ways the locus of family unity, encompassing all generations, alive and dead. The altar houses the spirit tablets in which ancestral spirits are believed to reside. The tablets typically record the names, birth and death dates, and number of sons of each ancestor. The ancestors are addressed and treated as close family members and are informed of family news such as births, deaths, engagements, travel and business plans. Ideally, it is the forebears of the senior male who are represented on the altar, but under certain circumstances other tablets may be present. For example, in a family with no sons, a daughter may put her natal family's tablets on the family altar of her husband.

The tablets go back three to five generations. The ancestors are offered incense twice daily (those who offer it vary between cultures). On death-day anniversaries and special holidays, such as New Year and the Mid-Autumn festival, the ancestors may also be offered food, drink, spirit money ("money" bought for the purpose of ancestral sacrifice), and paper clothes. During the funerary ritual, the dead are provided with spirit money as well as useful items rendered in paper, such as cars, servants, houses, and domestic furnishings. When offered food and drink, ancestors are believed to consume the "essence" and leave the coarse material part for the family to enjoy. The paper goods and spirit money are burned so that they ascend to the ancestors in smoke. In return, ancestors grant blessings of fertility, good

Smoke from incense and offerings before the tomb of Fu Xi, the "Ancestor of the Human Race," in Zhoukou.

luck, and harmony to their descendants—such rituals not only ensure blessings for the living, but also proclaim the unity and strength of the family.

As each generation passes away, the oldest tablets are removed from the altar and placed in an ancestral hall used by several households of the same extended family. Here, devotion takes place to the ancestors as a group; attitudes are more formal and indicative of gratitude to the host of forebears rather than the emotional bond and close relationship toward the more recently departed. Manuals that codified correct procedure and the details of the setup of the family altar and the ancestral hall were made available to the general population.

Ideas about the exact nature of the soul enshrined in the spirit tablets are vague and the material boundaries between the living and the dead are fluid. Those who reside in this world and the next are composed of the same vital material (*qi*) in its *yin* and *yang* forms (see pp.8–9). There is no formal agreement on the number of souls a person has, but since ancient times in China it is believed that everyone has at least two—a *hun* soul, made up of *yang qi*, and a *po* soul, made up of *yin qi*. At death, the *hun*, which represents the spiritual and intellectual aspect of the soul, departs from the body and ascends, due to its *yang* nature; it ultimately comes to reside in the ancestral tablets. The *po* soul, as *yin* energy, sinks into the ground. It remains with the body so long as it has been buried with the proper rites and is propitiated by tomb offerings.

Ancestors are propitiated family spirits. Those who are not properly cared for after death—through neglect or a lack of descendants—and those who die prematurely or by violence, become ghosts; they are likened to bandits and vagrants of the spirit world and are considered to be dangerous, malevolent forces that need to be placated. An ancestor may become a troublesome spirit if the burial is not performed correctly, or if the death was irregular, or if the spirit is not propitiated, preventing the *hun* soul from rising to reside in the ancestral tablets and the *po* soul from descending into the grave. The spirit of the deceased will haunt the living as a ghost until appropriate measures have been taken.

Other concerns over death and the afterlife in the popular tradition reflect the syncretistic tendency of East Asian religions, encompassing numerous—and, in some cases, apparently contradictory—notions of the fate of the soul after death. Thus, although the *po* soul of the deceased is at the gravesite, it is also believed to descend into the underworld, or Hell, where it will be judged and tried for its sins by the infernal judiciary before being punished and, eventually, reincarnated. Despite the fact that the concept of Hell existed in pre-Buddhist China, notions of the fate of the soul after death are heavily influenced by such Buddhist beliefs as: *karma* (an individual's balance of accumulated merits and demerits); the king of Hell; and the different punishment levels of Hell, in which sinners suffer to redress their karmic imbalance before being reincarnated.

On entering Hell, souls are judged by the Ten Magistrates, depicted in the costumes of the old Chinese imperial judiciary, who preside over the Ten Tribunals of Hell, each of which tries different crimes. Families can speed the passage of their loved ones in Hell through offerings and good works, such as the chanting of Buddhist *sutra*s. Both Heaven and Hell are envisioned as bureaucracies, with officials who are the celestial counterparts of Confucian literati-officials of the earthly realm in attire, role, and behavior. Buddhist cosmology was combined with Confucian filial piety in stories such as that of Mulian. A monk with no children, Mulian would have been considered unfilial by Confucians. However, he proved his superior filial piety by rescuing his mother from the torments of the lowest level of Hell, which was accessible to him because of his advanced achievements in Buddhist meditation.

The use of shamans and spirit mediums is another example of how Confucian values are combined with other practices in the management of the relationship with the dead. Unhappy ancestors may be the cause of problems in families troubled by illness or bad luck. In such cases, shamans or mediums are employed to communicate the grievances of the dead, typically through utterances or spirit writing. Although calling upon these persons was discouraged by the élite, their widespread use throughout East Asia shows a popular means by which family harmony can be restored and familial duty to the dead can be rectified.

Rites for the dead continue today, although they are discouraged by the Communist Party, which promotes atheism—observance in Communist countries thus depends on the prevailing political atmosphere. Christians have challenged Confucian rites since the Jesuit missions in the sixteenth century, questioning whether ancestor veneration is merely memorial or whether it is spirit-worship. Current Catholic ruling allows the rituals so long as they are for remembrance; Protestant interpretations vary. But regardless of ruling, a large percentage of Christian East Asians continues these practices, which are central to their identity and tradition. In Japan, rites are conducted at the family's Buddhist altar, but the rationale for the practices reflects Confucian sensibilities. Rites for the dead are widely observed in South Korea, and many homes will have manuals on proper practices of ancestral rituals. Observance of these rituals is costly and time-consuming—in 1980 the Korean government promulgated the "Guideline for Family Rituals" to curb the expense of honoring ancestors. Although the law is in effect, practices continue relatively unchanged, for ancestral rites are a primary way of expressing filial piety and family unity.

Family Rituals by Zhu Xi

66 When a man of virtue builds a house his first task
is always to set up an offering hall to the east of the
main room of his house. For this hall four altars to
hold the spirit tablets of the ancestors are made;
collateral relatives who died without descendants may
have associated offerings made to them there according
to their generational seniority. Sacrificial fields should
be established and sacrificial utensils prepared. Once
the hall is completed, early each morning the master
enters the outer gate to pay a visit. All comings and
goings are reported there. On New Year's Day, the
solstices and each new and full moon, visits are made.
On the customary festivals, seasonal foods are offered,
and when an event occurs, reports are made. Should
there be flood, fire, robbers, or bandits, the offering
hall is the first thing to be saved. The spirit tablets,
inherited manuscripts, and then the sacrificial utensils
should be moved; only afterward may the family's
valuables be taken. As one generation succeeds another,
the spirit tablets are reinscribed and moved to their
new places. **99**

From *Chu Hsi's Family Rituals*, translated by Patricia Buckley Ebrey. Princeton University Press: Princeton,
1991, p.5.

Commentary

Classic books of ritual practice such as the *Record of Rites* were valued in the Confucian tradition because they represented the wisdom of the ancients, and because they were guides to orthodox ritual behavior. However, there were practical difficulties involved in following their prescriptions due to the fact that they were derived from Chinese antiquity. Aware that such rites were too complicated and expensive for most people, and anxious to avoid divergent rites, the twelfth-century scholar Zhu Xi prepared the practical handbook *Family Rituals* as a resource for discouraging irregular practices and ensuring that essential rituals were performed properly.

Family Rituals outlines the four major family rituals: weddings, coming-of-age ceremonies, funerals, and ancestor veneration. Nearly half of the text discusses death ceremonies, including burial procedures and the complex rituals that were conducted to transform the dead into ancestors. Versions of Zhu Xi's text were tremendously popular and influential throughout East Asia, perhaps reflecting the existence of a widespread desire among the public for a ritual manual. The guidelines that were established in *Family Rituals* still form the basis of ancestor veneration in Korea today.

CHAPTER NINE

SOCIETY AND RELIGION

Confucianism has played a prominent role in shaping the social norms and expectations of East Asian society. Although integration with indigenous traditions and historical and geographical factors have given rise to variations in its influence, the tradition has nevertheless been an ordering principle of the family, the state, and social structure.

The patterns of influence of Confucianism have changed dramatically in the last 150 years. Social upheaval and encounters with the West have undoubtedly thrown into question its viability in the modern world. To some, the end of explicitly Confucian states has meant the death of Confucianism. But others believe there is evidence that the tradition is too strong to be broken altogether, despite the sometimes severe strains placed upon it.

LEFT: The three towering figures in East Asia's religious and philosophical traditions are brought together in this 18th-century Chinese painting. Confucius (right) holds the infant Buddha, while the Daoist sage Laozi looks on.

Confucianism has shaped East Asian social expectations and norms to such an extent that many cultural attitudes drawn from Confucian precepts are designated as being simply part of the cultural and national identity, rather than from a specific religious tradition. East Asian religions are a blend of many different traditions, and of these, Confucianism has remained the dominant influence in the realms of socialization, social structure, and ideals and practice of government.

In keeping with the Confucian ethic of filial piety, the primary relationship in East Asian society is that between parent and child. Traditionally, children owed their parents absolute loyalty and obedience. Chinese law reflected this relationship: for example, a father was within his rights to kill a disobedient child, and a son could be executed for striking his father. Children were expected to care for parents in their old age, to produce descendants who would continue the family line, and to perform ancestral rites.

Confucianism also provided the rationale for an authoritarian and hierarchical social structure in which males were highly privileged. In Confucian thought, each member of the family and of society had a specific role. In the Chinese view of the universe, women were considered embodiments of *yin* energy, and therefore passive and nurturing, in contrast to the dynamic *yang* of males (see pp.8–9). According to this scheme, they were subordinate to men and were expected to live in obedience to their fathers when girls, to their husbands when married, and to their sons when widowed. A married woman was supposed to show filial devotion to her husband's parents, with whom the couple often lived.

Confucianism's impact on society was especially significant in the realm of government. In China, emperors were understood to rule with the "Mandate of Heaven" (see p.13)—Heaven's sanction was endowed upon a virtuous and able leader who could benefit the people and pacify all under Heaven. Emperors were given the title "Son of Heaven," and through their ritual actions expressed their filiality and obedience to ancestors, and Heaven and Earth. The emperor was assisted by cultured, educated bureaucrats steeped in Confucian ethics. This system assumed that a centralized bureaucracy was the ordained manner of rule.

Confucius is revered as the first teacher, and his followers throughout the centuries have made education a high priority. In China, even the poorest people strove to educate their sons in the hope that at least one would pass the civil service examinations, bringing prestige and influence to their family.

Beijing Opera, one of the highest expressions of Chinese culture, includes lessons about Confucian ethics in its stories.

After serving as the theoretical basis for government and morality for two millennia, Confucianism came under attack as stiflingly traditional and as the underlying cause of China's political and military weakness. But since the beginning of the twentieth century, Confucian attitudes and orientations have come to accommodate modernity. This is apparent in Taiwan, Hong Kong, Singapore, and many overseas communities where Confucianism is often actively promoted. It is still evident in mainland China where Communism has imposed its own pressures, often in the form of severe persecution. However, although successive Communist leaders have vilified Confucianism, official rhetoric about working for the good of the state, party, or collective, and submitting to its authority, is not different in kind from the traditional Confucian emphasis on the group over the individual. In recent years, official pressure from the Communist Party has lessened and Confucianism is even promoted, mainly for its historical interest and value to tourism.

The strong emphasis on family unity and the relationship between child and parent continues in mainland China, although it has lessened in degree. It came under severe strain during the Cultural Revolution (1966–76), when Mao Zedong encouraged children and juniors to denounce the ways of their elders and seniors as "feudal" and counter-revolutionary. This experience, so profoundly opposed to the tradition of filial piety, undoubtedly left deep psychological scars. Even in the officially egalitarian People's Republic, there is still a marked preference for sons over daughters—the Communist policy of allowing couples only one child to counter overpopulation has given rise to a range of methods to ensure that the child is male.

South Koreans have had a different history. The Choson dynasty, which ended in 1910, saw perhaps the most distinctly Confucian state in history. The Confucian heritage in South Korea is still evident in patterns of daily life. The tremendous economic growth of the region has been fueled in part by the language of loyalty and obligations, where workers and citizens are called to sacrifice for the good of the company or the state. Families have a remarkably low divorce rate, and still prize the male family line and the need for male heirs. Practice of ancestral rites is widespread. An overwhelming percentage of the population, even among those who identify themselves as Christian, practices Confucian rituals and ceremonies, primarily in the form of ancestor veneration. There also continues to be a range of Confucian associations—from local Confucian temples to Seongkyunkwan University in Seoul. Groups such as *yurim*, or Confucian Forest, study and locally promote Confucian learning.

Vietnamese rulers, even when independent of Chinese control, followed the Confucian model of government and social order, including issuing imperial edicts of Confucian virtue for the populace and honoring filial sons and chaste wives. The Vietnamese retained distinctive aspects of their southeast Asian culture as well, sometimes to the disapproval of Chinese observers. In the nineteenth and twentieth centuries, with colonization by the French and the rise of Communism, Confucianism was no longer the foundation of state ideology, but continued to be the basis for social interaction. Since the Vietnam War and massive emigration, there has been disjuncture between the experience of generations—the expectations of the older generation are not always fulfilled by the younger.

The Japanese pattern is more diffuse than that of either Korea or Vietnam. The Japanese imported Confucianism with other aspects of Chinese culture in the sixth century. For them, Confucianism provided support to a centralized state and social hierarchy. However, once the basic elements were established, for many centuries Confucianism became a backdrop rather than a conscious pattern of life. Confucian studies were revived in the seventeenth century and again in the nineteenth century as a means of justifying the political and social hierarchy. Most notably, Confucianism was combined with aspects of Shinto in the period leading up to and during World War II to conflate loyalty to the emperor with filial piety to parents. Since the war, Confucian ideas have again become a part of the background to being Japanese, visible in the workplace, at school, and in gender roles and family structure.

Instructions for the Inner Quarters by Empress Xu

❝ Being upright and modest, reserved and quiet, correct
and dignified, sincere and honest: these constitute the
moral nature of a woman. Being filial and respectful,
humane and perspicacious, loving and warm, meek and
gentle: these represent the complete development of
the moral nature. The moral nature being innate in our
endowment, it becomes transformed and fulfilled
through practice. It is not something that comes from
the outside but is actually rooted in our very selves. . . .

The accumulation of small faults will mount
up to great harm to one's virtue. Therefore a great
house will topple over if the foundation is not solid.
One's moral nature will have deficiencies if the self
is not restrained.

Beautiful jade with no flaws can be made into
a precious jewel. An upright woman of pure character
can be made the wife of a great family. If you
constantly examine your actions to see if they are
correct, you can be a model mother. If you are hard-
working and frugal without a trace of jealousy, you are
fit to be an exemplar for the women's quarters. ❞

From *Neixun*, or "Instructions for the Inner Quarters," cited in S*ources of Chinese Tradition*, Vol. 1, compiled by
William Theodore de Bary and Irene Bloom. Columbia University Press: New York, 1999, pp. 834–35.

Commentary

In Confucian society, women were thought to be *yin*, like the earth, and thus to be passive and yielding. They nevertheless played a crucial role in the family: they were responsible for the early education and nurturing of children, and for remonstrating with husbands who erred. Many illustrious figures credited female family members for having contributed to their achievements. One famous example was Mencius' mother, who moved three times with her son to ensure that he grew up in surroundings that would nurture moral and intellectual growth.

Many manuals for the "inner quarters" were written by highly educated and accomplished women. These books gave guidance on following the "wifely Way": sacrificing to ancestors, caring for parents-in-law, and bearing children. This extract from the *Instructions for the Inner Quarters* (written in the Ming dynasty by Empress Xu, and well received in Korea and Japan as well as China) affirms the Confucian teachings of the "Great Learning," which asserts that one's own character must be developed in order to, ultimately, bring order to the world. It therefore describes not only a woman's domestic duties, but also the means for her self-cultivation, an achievement which contributes to the general good.

GLOSSARY

Chunqiu *Spring and Autumn Annals*, one of the Five Classics.

Dong Zhongshu 2nd-century BCE (Han Dynasty) Confucian statesman and philosopher.

Kongzi, Kong Fuzi Master Kong; Confucius.

li 1. ritual, ceremony; 2. reason, principle, as in the pre-existing principles behind the world and all the objects in it. (In written Chinese these words are written with different characters.)

Li Ji *Record of Rites*, one of the Five Classics.

Mencius Latinized form of Mengzi, the major Ru philosopher of the 4th century BCE and interpreter of Confucius's ideas

Neo-Confucianism Confucian revival under the Song Dynasty, which incorporated elements of both Daoism and Buddhism.

qi vital matter; the material of which all things are made.

ren goodness, humaneness, magnanimity, the supreme virtue of a superior person (*junzi*).

Ru the school of philosophy founded by Confucius; Confucian scholar. From *ru*, meaning "weak' or "yielding."

Shi Jing *Classic of Poetry*, one of the Five Classics.

shu reciprocity; closely connected with the idea of *ren*.

Shu Jing *Classic of Documents*, one of the Five Classics.

Taiji the all-embracing *li* of the universe, the Great Ultimate.

Tian Heaven; emperors were believed to be mandated to rule by Heaven.

xiao filial piety; the cornerstone of family, and therefore social, order.

Xunzi a major Ru philosopher of the 3rd century BCE.

yang the aspect of *qi* that is light, masculinity and movement.

yi righteousness, honor, loyalty.

yin the aspect of *qi* that is darkness, femininity and quiescence.

Yi Jing *Classic of Changes*, one of the Five Classics.

zhong sincerity, the sentiment from which reciprocity (*shu)* springs.

Zhu Xi the 12th-century CE philosopher who expounded the revivalist movement known as Neo-Confucianism.

GENERAL BIBLIOGRAPHY

Birrell, Anne. *Chinese Mythology: An Introduction*. Baltimore: Johns Hopkins University Press, 1993.

Chan, Wing-tsit. *A Source Book in Chinese Philosophy*. Princeton: Princeton University Press, 1963.

Chu Hsi. *Learning to be a Sage*. Berkeley: University of California Press, 1990.

Confucius. *The Analects*. (D.C. Lau, trans.) New York: Viking, 1979.

De Bary, William Theodore, et al., eds. *Sources of Chinese Tradition*. Vols. 1 and 2, 2nd ed. New York: Columbia University Press, 1999.

Fingarette, Herbert. *Confucius: The Sacred as Secular*. New York: Harper & Row, 1972.

Fung Yu-lan. *A Short History of Chinese Philosophy*. New York: The Macmillan Company, 1948.

Graham, A.C. *Disputers of the Tao*. LaSalle, Illinois: Open Court Publishing Company, 1989.

I Ching. (Richard Wilhelm, trans., and from German to English by Cary F. Baynes.) 3rd ed. Princeton: Princeton University Press, 1967.

Jordan, David. *Gods, Ghosts, and Ancestors: The Folk Religion of a Taiwanese Village*. Berkeley: University of California Press, 1972.

Martin, Emily. *The Cult of the Dead in a Chinese Village*. Stanford: Stanford University Press, 1973.

Mencius. *The Mencius*. (D.C. Lau, trans.) Harmondsworth: Penguin, 1970.

Overmyer, Daniel L. *Religions of China: The World as a Living System*. San Francisco: Harper & Row, 1986.

Overmyer, Daniel L.; Alvin P. Cohen; N.J. Girardot and Wing-tsit Chan. "Chinese Religions" in *The Encyclopedia of Religion* (ed. Mircea Eliade), Vol. 3., pp. 257–323. New York: Macmillan, 1987.

Paper, Jordan and Thompson, Laurence. *The Chinese Way in Religion*. 2nd ed. Belmont, California: Wadsworth, 1998.

Pound, Ezra. *The Classical Anthology Defined by Confucius (The* Shi Jing *or Book of Songs)*. Cambridge, Massachusetts: Harvard University Press, 1954.

Stepanchuk, Carol and Wong, Charles. *Mooncakes and Hungry Ghosts: Festivals of China*. San Francisco: China Books and Periodicals, 1991.

Thompson, Laurence. *Chinese Religion: An Introduction*. 5th ed. Belmont, California: Wadsworth, 1998.

Tu Wei-ming. *Confucian Thought: Selfhood as Creative Transformation*. Albany: State University of NY Press, 1985.

Waley, Arthur. *The Analects of Confucius*. London: George Allen and Unwin, 1938.

Waley, Arthur. *The Book of Songs*. Boston and New York: Houghton Miflin, 1937.

Waley, Arthur. *Three Ways of Thought in Ancient China*. London: George Allen and Unwin, 1939.

Yang, C.K. *Religion in Chinese Society*. Berkeley and Los Angeles: University of California Press, 1961.

INDEX

Page numbers in **bold** refer to major references; page numbers in *italics* refer to captions

ACKNOWLEDGMENTS AND PICTURE CREDITS

Unless cited otherwise here, text extracts are out of copyright or the product of the author's own translation. The following sources have kindly given their permission.

Aspects of the Divine, p.30: from *A Source Book in Chinese Philosophy* by Wing-tsit Chan. Princeton University Press: Princeton, 1963, pp.497–98.

Sacred Space, pp.70–71: from *Sourcebook of Korean Civilization*, Vol. 1, edited by Peter H. Lee. Columbia University Press: New York, 1993, pp.523–24.

Death and the Afterlife, p.94: from *Chu Hsi's Family Rituals*, translated by Patricia Buckley Ebrey. Princeton University Press: Princeton, 1991, p.5.

Society and Religion, p.104: from *Sources of Chinese Tradition*, Vol. 1, compiled by William Theodore de Bary and Irene Bloom. Columbia University Press: New York, 1999, pp.834–35.

The publisher would like to thank the following people, museums, and photographic libraries for permission to reproduce their material. Every care has been taken to trace copyright holders. However, if we have omitted anyone we apologize, and will, if informed, make corrections in any future edition. **Page 2** Hutchison Library, London/Trevor Page; **7** British Museum, London; **10** British Museum, London; **16** Bridgeman Art Library, London/Bibliothèque Nationale, Paris; **24** Bridgeman Art Library, London/Private Collection; **28** Corbis/Dean Conger; **32** Art Archive, London/ Bibliotheque Nationale, Paris; **38** DBP; **42** DBP/John Chinnery; **46** DBP/John Chinnery; **52** Art Archive, London/ Victoria & Albert Museum, London; **59** Art Archive, London/British Museum, London; **62** Hutchison Library, London; **66** Hutchison Library, London/Michael Macintyre; **72** Corbis/Mike Yamashita; **76** Panos Pictures, London/ Mark Henley; **84** Bridgeman Art Library, London/Private Collection; **89** Panos Pictures, London/Mark Henley; **96** Art Archive, London/British Museum, London; **100** Hutchison Library,m London/Michael Macintyre.